Table of Contents

Rourke
Educational Media
rourkeeducationalmedia.com

Can you find these words?

goalie

puck

skates

teammate

Let's Play!

I play ice hockey.

3

skates

I wear ice **skates.**
I wear a helmet.

4

I wear kneepads and gloves.

I skate across the ice.

I move the **puck** with my stick.

puck

I pass the puck to my **teammate**.
She shoots the puck.

teammate

goalie

The puck goes past the **goalie.**

It goes in the net.
We score a point!

Sometimes we win.
Sometimes we lose.

We always have fun!

Did you find these words?

The puck goes past the **goalie**.

I move the **puck** with my stick.

I wear ice **skates**.

I pass the puck to my **teammate**.

Photo Glossary

 **goalie** (GOH-lee): Someone who guards the goal to keep the other team from scoring.

 **puck** (puhk): A hard, round, flat piece of rubber used in ice hockey.

 **skates** (skayts): Boots with blades fastened to the sole used for gliding on ice.

 **teammate** (teem-mate): Someone who is a member of your team.

Index

About the Author

Elliot Riley is the author of dozens of books for kids. When she's not reading or writing, you can find her walking by the water in sunny Tampa, Florida.

www.rourkeeducationalmedia.com

PHOTO CREDITS: Cover: ©Volkovalrina; p2,5,6,7,10,11,14,15: ©bigjohn36; p2,7,14,15: ©gilaxia; p2,4,14,15: ©nicole waring; p3: ©A330Pilot; p11: ©Valeriy Lebedev; p13: ©francisblack

Edited by: Keli Sipperley
Cover by: Rhea Magaro-Wallace
Interior design by: Kathy Walsh

Library of Congress PCN Data
Ice Hockey / Elliot Riley
(Ready for Sports)
ISBN 978-1-64369-053-7 (hard cover)(alk. paper)
ISBN 978-1-64369-085-8 (soft cover)
ISBN 978-1-64369-200-5 (e-Book)
Library of Congress Control Number: 2018955846

Printed in the United States of America, North Mankato, Minnesota